Book One

On The Farm • Kids & Critters • Storybook Characters

Draw • Write • NOW®

by
Marie Hablitzel
and
Kim Stitzer

*A Drawing
and Handwriting
Course for Kids!*

Barker Creek Publishing, Inc. • Poulsbo, Washington

Dedicated to...

...my grandchildren.
I have enjoyed drawing with you! — M.H.

...Randy, Michelle, and Ty. — K.S.

The text on the handwriting pages is set in a custom
font created from Marie Hablitzel's handwriting.
The drawings are done using Prismacolor pencils
outlined with a black PaperMate FLAIR!® felt tip pen.

BARKER CREEK

Published by Barker Creek Publishing, Inc.
P.O. Box 2610 • Poulsbo, WA 98370-2610
800•692•5833 FAX: 360•613•2542
barkercreek.com

Book layout by Judy Richardson
Printed in Hong Kong

Library of Congress Catalog Card Number: 93-73893

Publisher's Cataloging in Publication Data:
Hablitzel, Marie, 1920 -
Draw•Write•Now®, Book One: A drawing and handwriting course for kids!
(first in series)

Summary: A collection of drawing and handwriting lessons for children. *Book One* focuses on farm life, children, pets and storybook characters. First book in the *Draw•Write•Now®* series.

1. Drawing—Technique—Juvenile Literature. 2. Drawing—Study and Teaching (Elementary).   3. Penmanship.
4. Farm Life—Juvenile Literature.
I. Stitzer, Kim, 1956 -   , coauthor. II. Title.
741.2   [372.6]

ISBN: 0-9639307-1-0

Eighth Printing

About this book...

For most children, drawing is their first form of written communication. Long before they master the alphabet and sentence syntax, children express themselves creatively on paper through line and color.

As children mature, their imaginations often race ahead of their drawing skills. By teaching them to see complex objects as combinations of simple shapes and encouraging them to develop their fine-motor skills through regular practice, they can better record the images they see so clearly in their minds.

This book contains a collection of beginning drawing lessons and text for practicing handwriting. These lessons were developed by a teacher who saw her second-grade students becoming increasingly frustrated with their drawing efforts and disenchanted with repetitive handwriting drills.

For more than 30 years, Marie Hablitzel refined what eventually became a daily drawing and handwriting curriculum. Marie's premise was simple —drawing and handwriting require many of the same skills. And, regular practice in a supportive environment is the key to helping children develop

Coauthors Marie Hablitzel (left) and her daughter, Kim Stitzer

their technical skills, self-confidence and creativity. As a classroom teacher, Marie intertwined her daily drawing and handwriting lessons with math, science, social studies, geography, reading and creative writing. She wove an educational tapestry that hundreds of children have found challenging, motivating — and fun!

Although Marie is now retired, her drawing and handwriting lessons continue to be used in the classroom. With the assistance of her daughter, Kim Stitzer, Marie shares more than 150 of her lessons in the eight-volume *Draw•Write•Now®* series.

In *Draw•Write•Now®, Book One*, children explore life on a farm, kids and critters and storybook characters. *Books Two* through *Six* feature topics as diverse as Christopher Columbus, the weather, Native Americans, the polar regions, young Abraham Lincoln, beaver ponds and life in the sea. In *Draw•Write•Now®, Books Seven and Eight*, children circle the globe while learning about animals of the world.

We hope your children and students enjoy these lessons as much as ours have!

—*Carolyn Hurst, Publisher*

Look for these books in the *Draw•Write•Now,* series...

Book One: On the Farm, Kids and Critters, Storybook Characters
Book Two: Christopher Columbus, Autumn Harvest, The Weather
Book Three: Native Americans, North America, The Pilgrims
Book Four: The Polar Regions, The Arctic, The Antarctic
Book Five: The United States, From Sea to Sea, Moving Forward
Book Six: Animals & Habitats: On Land, Ponds and Rivers, Oceans
Book Seven: Animals of the World, Part I: Forest Animals
Book Eight: Animals of the World, Part II: Grassland and Desert Animals

For additional information call 1-800-692-5833 or visit barkercreek.com

Table of Contents

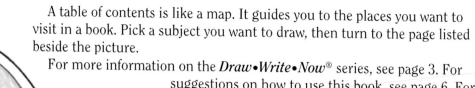

A table of contents is like a map. It guides you to the places you want to visit in a book. Pick a subject you want to draw, then turn to the page listed beside the picture.

For more information on the *Draw•Write•Now*® series, see page 3. For suggestions on how to use this book, see page 6. For a review of handwriting tips, see page 8.

On the Farm Page 9

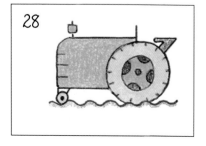 

Kids and Critters   Page 33

34

36

38

40

42

44

46

48

50

Storybook Characters   Page 51

52

54

56

58

60

62

Teaching Tips   Page 63

5

A few tips to get started...

This is a book for children and their parents, teachers and caregivers. Although most young people can complete the lessons in this book quite successfully on their own, a little help and encouragement from a caring adult can go a long way toward building a child's self-confidence, creativity and technical skills.

*South American Llama by Michelle Stitzer, age 7
from Draw•Write•Now®, Book Seven*

The following outline contains insights from the 30-plus years the authors have worked with the material in this book. Realizing that no two children or classrooms are alike, the authors encourage you to modify these lessons to best suit the needs of your child or classroom. Each *Draw•Write•Now®* lesson includes five parts:

    1. Introduce the subject.
    2. Draw the subject.
    3. Draw the background.
    4. Practice handwriting.
    5. Color the drawing.

As presented here, each child will need a pencil, an eraser, drawing paper, penmanship paper and either crayons, color pencils or felt tip markers to complete a lesson.

1. Introduce the Subject
Begin the lesson by generating interest in the subject with a story, discussion, poem, photograph or song. The questions on the illustrated notes scattered throughout this book are examples of how interest can be built along a related theme. Answers to these questions and the titles of several theme-related books are on pages 32, 50 and 62.

2. Draw the Subject
Have the children draw with a pencil. Encourage them to draw lightly because some lines (shown as dashed lines on the drawing lessons) will need to be erased. Show the children the finished drawing in the book. Point out the shapes and lines in the subject as the children work through the lesson. Help the children see that complex objects can be viewed as combinations of lines and simple shapes.

Help the children be successful! Show them how to position the first step on their papers in an appropriate size. Initially, the children may find some shapes difficult to draw. If they do, provide a pattern for them to trace, or draw the first step for them. Once they fine-tune their skills and build their self-confidence, their ability and creativity will take over. For lesson-specific drawing tips and suggestions, refer to *Teaching Tips* on pages 63–64.

3. Draw the Background
Encourage the children to express their creativity and imagination in the backgrounds they add to their pictures. Add to their creative libraries by demonstrating various ways to draw trees, horizons and other details. Point out background details in the drawings in this book, illustrations from other books, photographs and works of art.

Encourage the children to draw their world by looking for basic shapes and lines in the things they see around them. Ask them to draw from their imaginations by using their developing skills. For additional ideas on motivating children to draw creatively, see pages 30–31, 48–49 and 60–61.

4. Practice Handwriting
In place of drills—rows of e's, r's and so on—it is often useful and more motivating to have children write complete sentences when practicing their handwriting. When the focus is on handwriting—

rather than spelling or vocabulary enrichment—use simple words that the children can easily read and spell. Begin by writing each word with the children, demonstrating how individual letters are formed and stressing proper spacing. Start slowly. One or two sentences may be challenging enough in the beginning. Once the children are consistently forming their letters correctly, encourage them to work at their own pace.

There are many ways to adapt these lessons for use with your child or classroom. For example, you may want to replace the authors' text with your own words. You may want to let the children compose sentences to describe their drawings or answer the theme-related questions found throughout the book. You may prefer to replace the block alphabet used in this book with a cursive, D'Nealian® or other alphabet style. If you are unfamiliar with the various alphabet styles used for teaching handwriting, consult your local library. A local elementary school may also be able to recommend an appropriate alphabet style and related resource materials.

5. Color the Picture

Children enjoy coloring their own drawings. The beautiful colors, however, often cover the details they have so carefully drawn in pencil. To preserve their efforts, you may want to have the children trace their pencil lines with black crayons or fine-tipped felt markers.

Crayons—When coloring with crayons, have the children outline their drawings with a black crayon

Eskimo by Marianne Hablitzel, age 8
from Draw•Write•Now®, Book Four

Fish by Sam Hablitzel, age 6
from Draw•Write•Now®, Book Six

after they have colored their pictures (the black crayon may smear if they do their outlining first).

Color Pencils—When coloring with color pencils, have the children outline their drawings with a felt tip marker *before* they color their drawings.

Felt Tip Markers—When coloring with felt tip markers, have the children outline their drawings with a black marker *after* they have colored their pictures.

Your comments are appreciated!
How are you sharing Draw•Write•Now® with your children or students? The authors would appreciate hearing from you. Write to Marie Hablitzel and Kim Stitzer, c/o Barker Creek Publishing, P.O. Box 2610, Poulsbo, WA 98370, USA or visit our website at www.barkercreek.com.

"Batter up!" by Tyler Stitzer, age 5
from Draw•Write•Now®, Book One

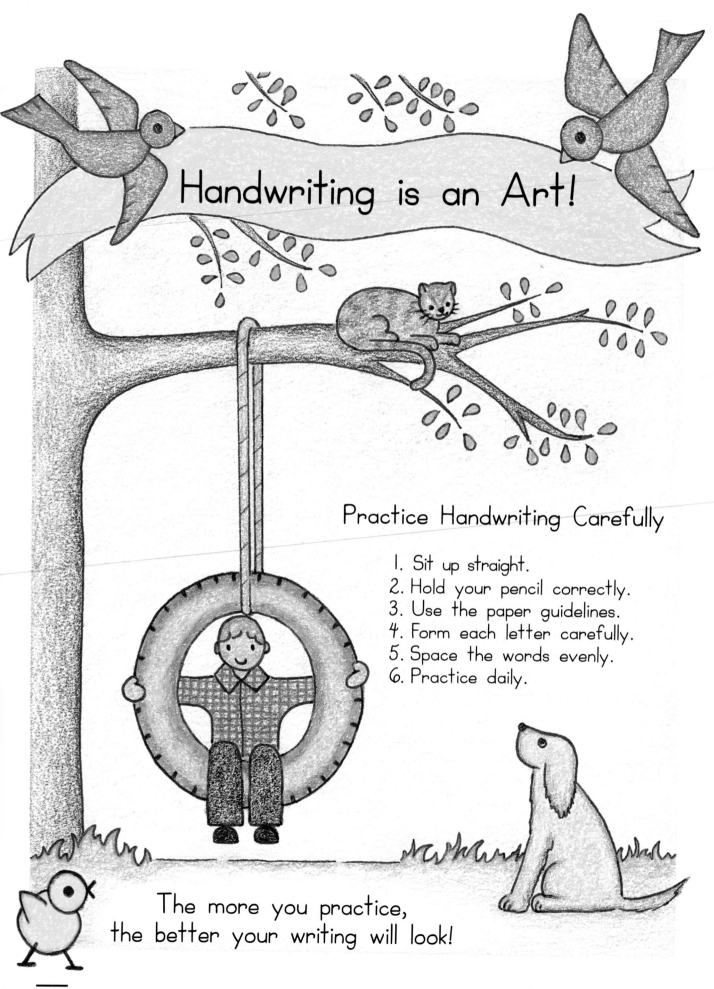

Handwriting is an Art!

Practice Handwriting Carefully

1. Sit up straight.
2. Hold your pencil correctly.
3. Use the paper guidelines.
4. Form each letter carefully.
5. Space the words evenly.
6. Practice daily.

The more you practice,
the better your writing will look!

On the Farm

Hens live on farms.

Hens eat seeds.

Hens lay eggs.

Hens have baby chicks.

How does a chick grow inside an egg?

Question answered on page 32

1.
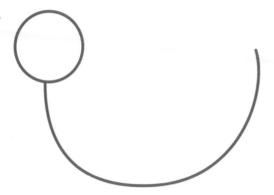

2.
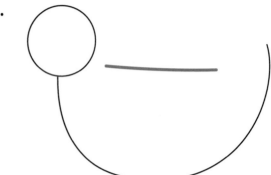

3.
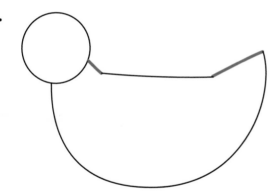

4.
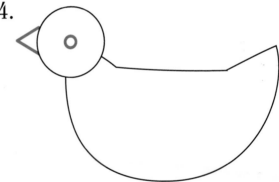

5.

6.

Pig

Teaching Tip on page 64
Question answered on page 32

1.

2.

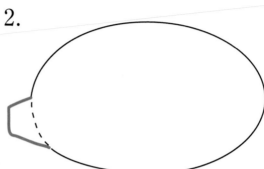

3.

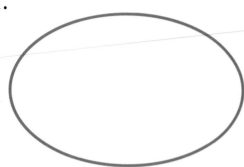

4.

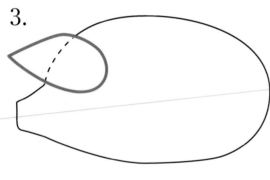

5.

6.

Pigs live on farms.
They stay in pens.
They like corn.
Pigs play in mud.

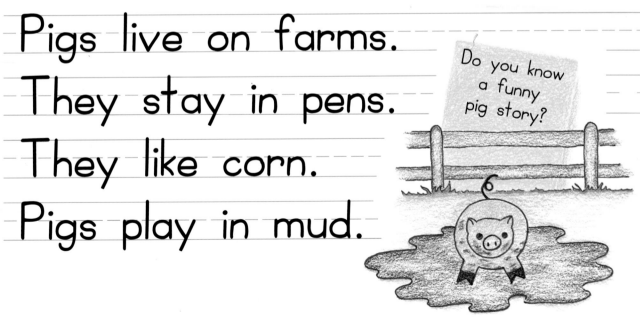

Do you know a funny pig story?

Sheep live on farms.
Sheep eat grass.
Some sheep are white.
Sheep have wool.

How is wool made into clothes?

Sheep

Teaching Tip on page 64
Question answered on page 32

1.

2.

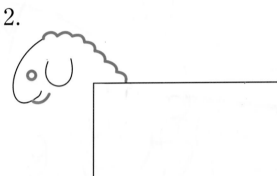

3.

4.

5.

6.

Cow

Teaching Tip on page 64
Question answered on page 32

1.

2.

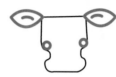

3.

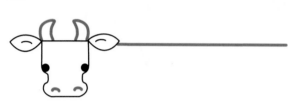

4.

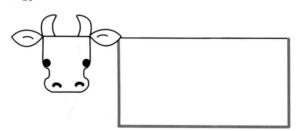

5.

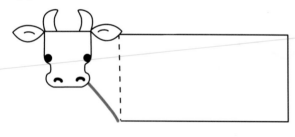

6.

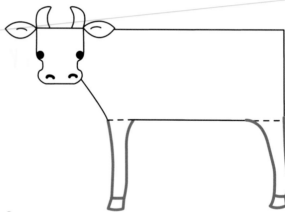

7.

8.

Cows live on farms.
Cows sleep in barns.
They eat grass.
They give us milk.

How do cows make milk?

Horses live on farms.
Horses eat grass.
Horses run fast.
We ride horses.

How were horses used on farms 100 years ago?

Horse

Teaching Tip on page 64
Question answered on page 32

1.

2.

3.

4.

5.

6.

7.

8.

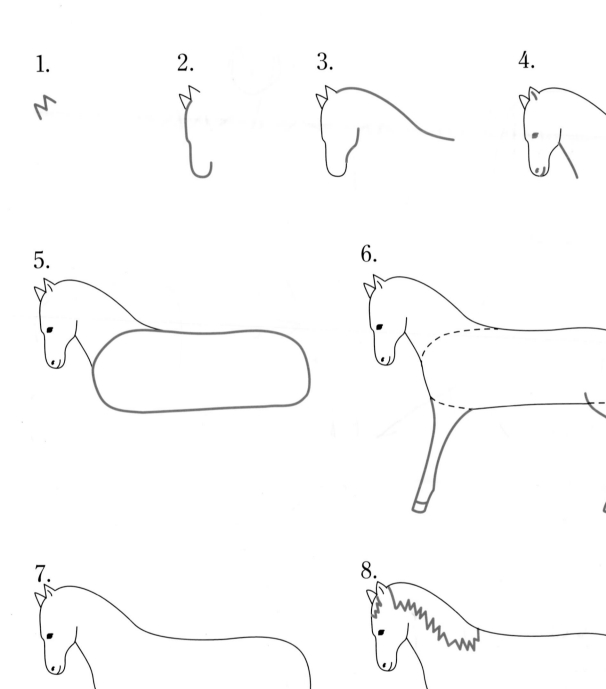

Turkey

1.

2.

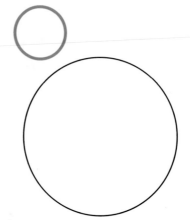

3.

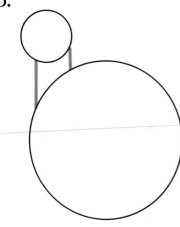

4.

5.

6.

Farmers raise turkeys.
Turkeys are big birds.
We hear them gobble.
They are noisy.

We see barns on farms.
Animals live in barns.
Hay is kept in barns.
Barns have big doors.

Why do barns have big doors?

Barn

Teaching Tip on page 64
Question answered on page 32

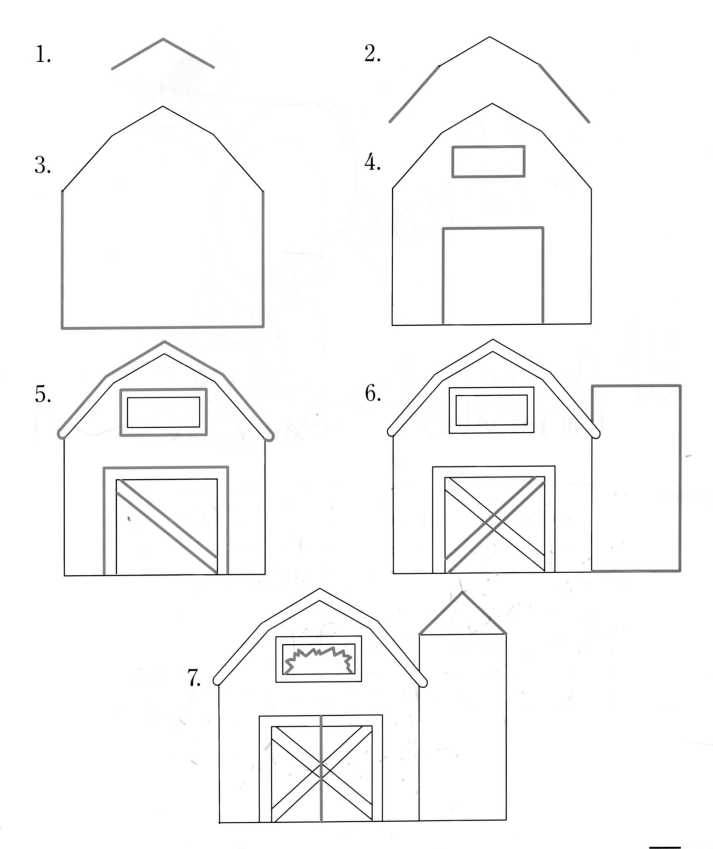

1.

2.

3.

4.

5.

6.

7.

Duck

Teaching Tip on page 64
Question answered on page 32

1.

2.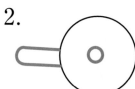

3.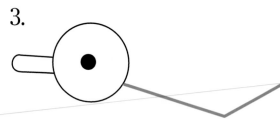

4.

Ducks like the water.
They swim in it.
They play in it.
They have webbed feet.

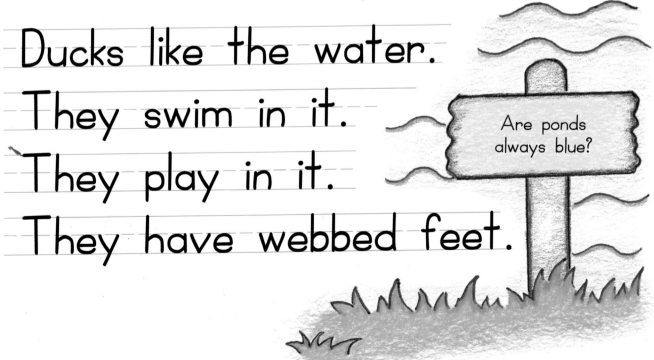

Are ponds always blue?

Some farms have geese.
Geese are bigger than ducks.
They have feet like ducks.
They lay eggs.

What do wild geese see when they fly over farms?

Goose

Question answered on page 32

1.

2.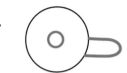

3.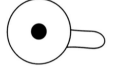

4.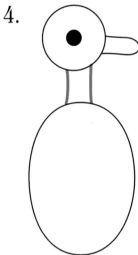

5.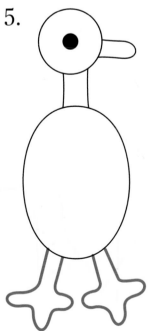

6.

Tractor

Teaching Tip on page 64
Question answered on page 32

1.

2.

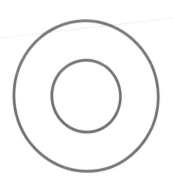

3.

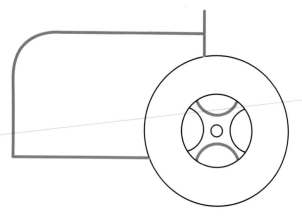

4.

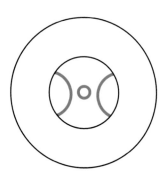

5.

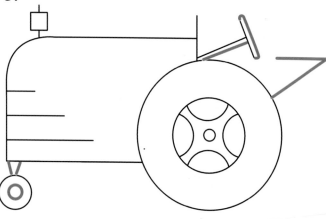

6.

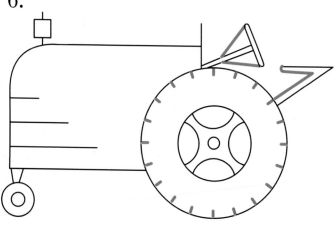

Tractors help the farmer.
Tractors work in fields.
Tractors pull loads.
Tractors are noisy.

How did farmers plow their fields before they had tractors?

Draw What You See

Where have you seen farm animals?

By mountains?

At a fair?

Near woods?

In a parade?

Kids and Critters

Jumping rope is fun.
Jump rope fast or slow.
Try jumping with a friend.
Start a jump rope team.

Do you know some jump rope tricks?

1.

2.

3.

4.

5.

6.

Boy

1.

b o y

2.

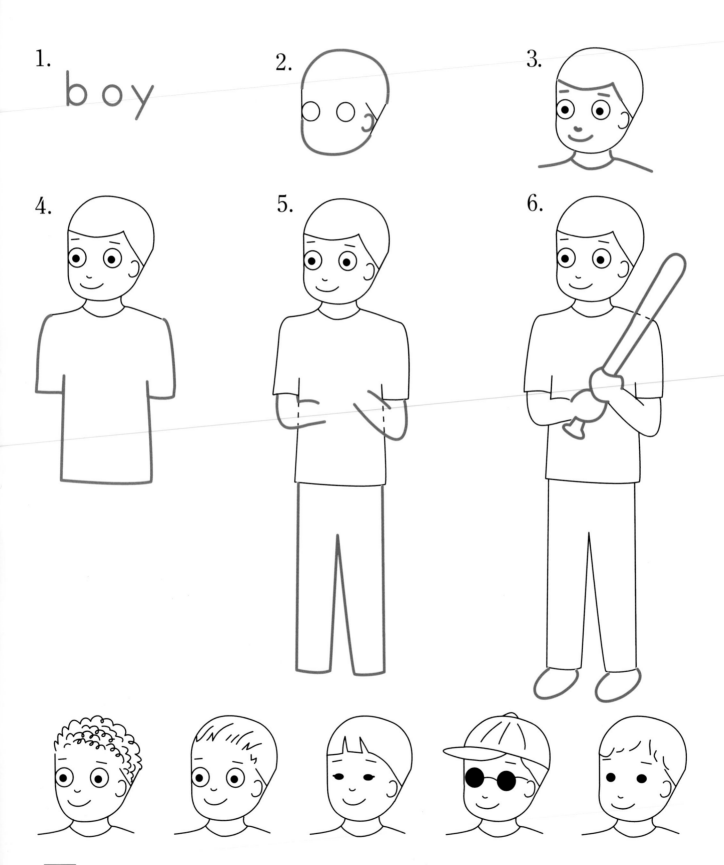

3.

4.

5.

6.

Baseball is a fun game.

The pitcher throws the ball.

The batter hits the ball.

The fielders try to catch it.

Cats make good pets.
They drink milk.
They have soft fur.
They catch mice.

Do mice make good pets?

Cat

Question answered on page 50

1.

2.

3.

4.

5.

6.

Dog

1.

2.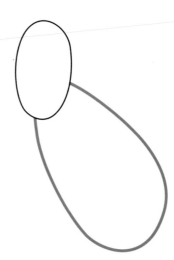

3.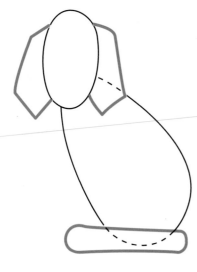

4.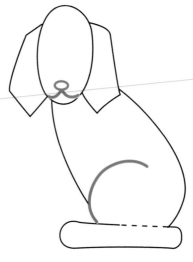

5.

6.

Dogs are good pets.
We like to play with dogs.
Dogs may be big or small.
They wag their tails.

Swan

Teaching Tip on page 64

1.

2.

3.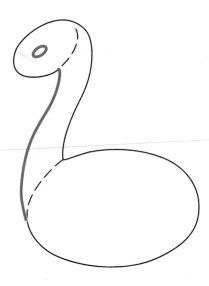

4.

5.

6.

Swans are big birds.
They swim in the water.
Some lakes have swans.
Swans are pretty birds.

Rabbits are furry.
They hop and leap.
They hear very well.
They eat plants.

Why are rabbits different colors?

Rabbits

Question answered on page 50

1.

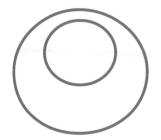

2.

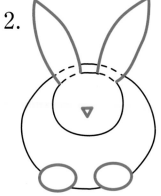

3.

4.

1.

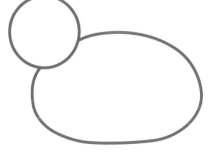

2.

3.

4.

Draw Your World

Where do you like to play?

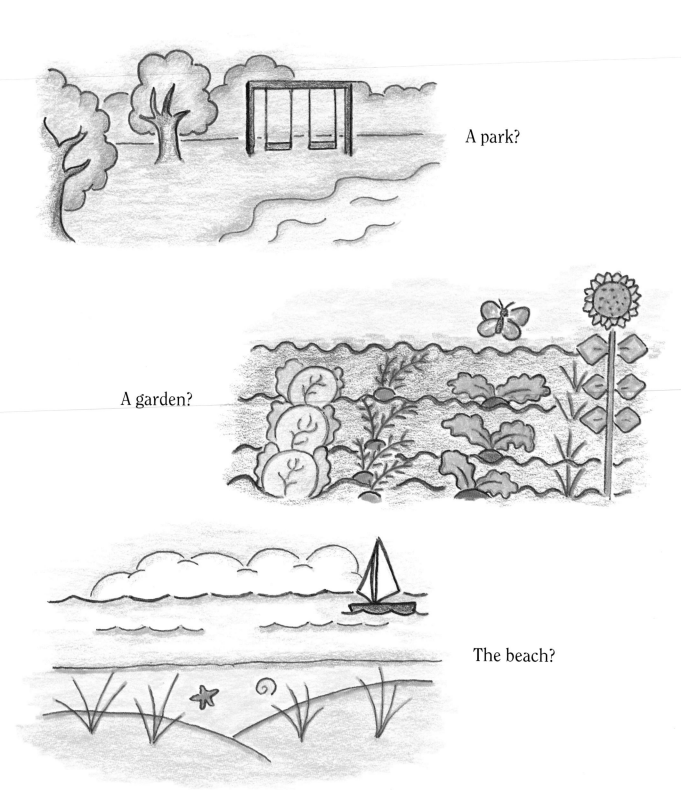

A park?

A garden?

The beach?

Do the trees and plants near your home look like these?

Trees
(pages 13, 22, 25, 26, 37 and 38)

Flowers
(page 34)

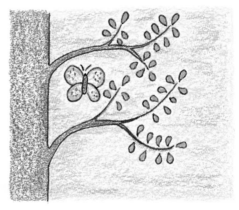

Branches and Leaves
(page 42)

Bushes
(pages 10 and 46)

Reeds and Grasses
(pages 13, 41, 45, 52 and 55)

Learn more about kids and critters...

DO YOU KNOW SOME JUMP ROPE TRICKS? Page 34

Learn the Criss-Cross, The Wheel, jump rope rhymes and games in RED HOT PEPPERS *by Bob Boardman, illustrated by Diane Boardman, published by Sasquatch Books and Skookum Jump Rope Co., 1993.*

DO MICE MAKE GOOD PETS? Page 38

Many people enjoy pet mice. Can you imagine a cat keeping mice as pets? That's what happens in MARTIN'S MICE *by Dick King-Smith, illustrated by Jez Alborough, published by Dell, 1988. Martin, a farm cat, loves his pet mice (even if they do complain too much). One day, a woman takes Martin to her home in the city so he can be* **her** *pet. Does Martin like being a pet?*

WHAT COLOR ARE THE BIRDS NEAR YOUR HOME? Page 42

Birdwatching is fun! Go along with someone who knows and enjoys birds—Crinkleroot! Crinkleroot is an old woodsman with tips for beginning birdwatchers of all ages in CRINKLEROOT'S GUIDE TO KNOWING THE BIRDS *written and illustrated by Jim Arnosky, published by Macmillan, 1992.*

WHY ARE RABBITS DIFFERENT COLORS? Page 46

Color camouflages rabbits. In the wild, white rabbits live in snowy places, gray rabbits live in dark forests and tan rabbits live in dusty, dry places. To see how camouflage protects rabbits, read RABBITS IN THE MEADOW *written and photographed by Lilo Hess, published by T.Y. Crowell Co., 1963.*

HERE ARE SOME BOOKS ABOUT CHILDREN...

THE REAL HOLE *by Beverly Cleary, illustrated by DyAnne DiSalvo-Ryan, published by W. Morrow, 1986. Jimmy dug a hole. No one knew he could dig such a deep hole. What will he do with it?*

JASON'S BUS RIDE *by Harriet Ziefert, illustrated by Simms Taback, published by Puffin Books, 1987. A dog was in front of the bus. He would not get out of the way. How will Jason help?*

ROXABOXEN *by Alice McLerran, illustrated by Barbara Cooney, published by Lothrop, Lee & Shepard, 1991. The children play on a hill covered with rocks, old boxes and cacti. What makes the hill so fun?*

GALIMOTO *by Karen Lynn Williams, illustrated by Catherine Stock, published by Lothrop, Lee & Shepard, 1990. Kondi wants to build a toy car made of wire. But first, he must get wire. Can he build the car?*

SWEET CLARA AND THE FREEDOM QUILT *by Deborah Hopkinson, illustrated by James Ransome, published by Knopf, 1993. Clara is a slave. To be free, she must walk far. She is strong enough to walk, but she has no map. How will she find her way?*

HAROLD AND THE PURPLE CRAYON *written and illustrated by Crockett Johnson, published by HarperCollins, 1955. Harold walks into his drawings! He can draw a boat and ride in it. When he's hungry, he eats the food he draws. Can he draw his way back home?*

FEELINGS *written and illustrated by Aliki, published by Greenwillow, 1984. Happy. Sad. Sorry. Proud. Other children have these feelings. Do you?*

Storybook Characters

Red Hen planted a seed.

She raised some wheat.

She made the wheat into flour.

She made bread from the flour.

How is flour made?

Little Red Hen

Question answered on page 62

1.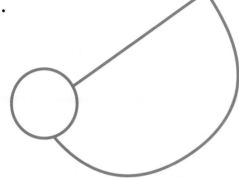

2.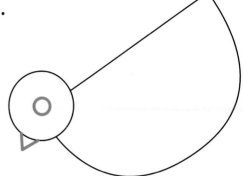

3.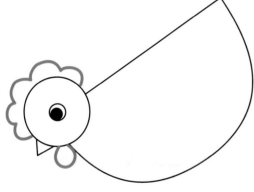

4.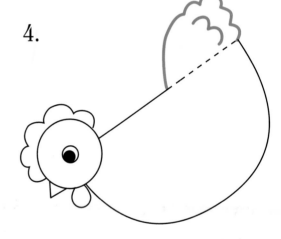

5.

6.

Three Little Pigs

Teaching Tip on page 64

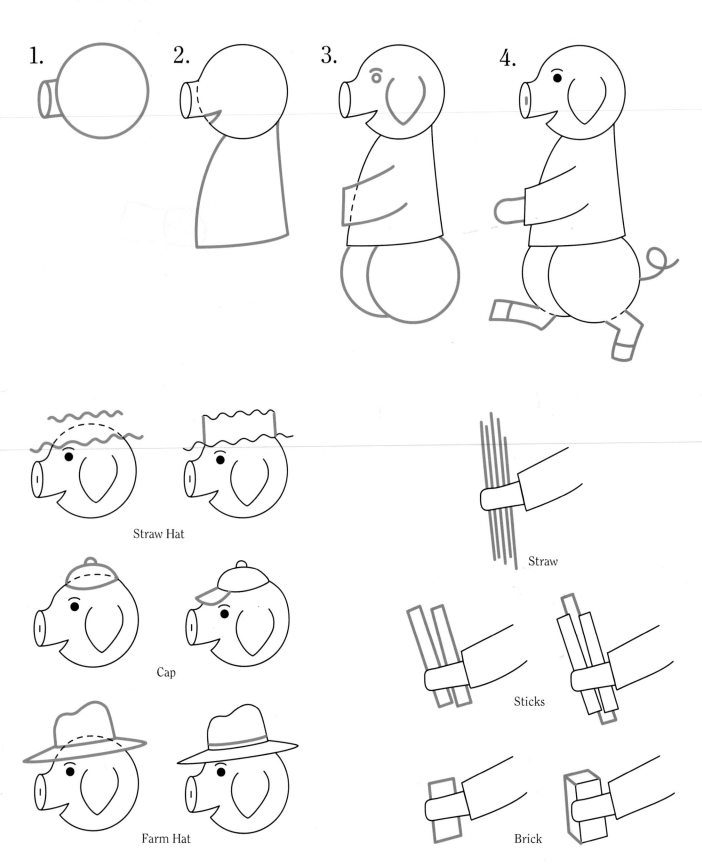

1.

2.

3.

4.

Straw Hat

Cap

Farm Hat

Straw

Sticks

Brick

Three little pigs built houses.

One was built of straw.

One was built of sticks.

One was built of bricks.

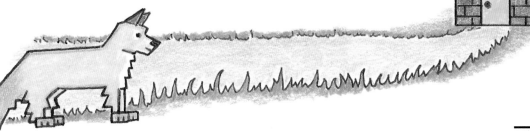

Father Bear's soup was too hot.
Mother Bear's soup was too cold.
Baby Bear's soup was just right.
Goldilocks ate all of it.

Three Bears

Teaching Tip on page 64

1.

2.

3.

Father Bear's Hat

Father Bear's Collar

Mother Bear's Hat

Mother Bear's Collar

Baby Bear's Hat

Baby Bear's Collar

Gingerbread Boy

Teaching Tip on page 64
Question answered on page 62

1.

2.

3.

4.

The gingerbread boy ran away.
The bear did not catch him.
The dog did not catch him.
The fox caught him.

Why is the gingerbread boy drawn bigger than the house?

Draw From Your Imagination

Tell your own story.

Where are the birds going?

What are the ducks saying?

Who is Nellie the Cow?

Draw different hats on the characters in your stories.

Pirate Hat

Firefighter's Hat

Rain Hat

Baker's Hat

Ranger's Hat

Stocking Cap

(see more hats on pages 55 and 56)

Hard Hat

Straw Hat

Sombrero

Sailor's Hat

Cowboy Hat

Cowboy Hat

Learn more from storybooks ...

HOW IS FLOUR MADE? Page 52

Flour is made from grain that has been crushed (ground) into small pieces. The most common flour is made from wheat, the same grain that the Little Red Hen used. Most people buy flour that has been ground in a flour mill. A flour mill can grind a lot of grain quickly. For another look at grinding wheat into flour, read Chapter 19 of THE LONG WINTER by Laura Ingalls Wilder, illustrated by Garth Williams, published by HarperCollins, 1953.

WHY IS THE GINGERBREAD BOY DRAWN BIGGER THAN THE HOUSE? Page 59

Things look big when they are near and small when they are far away. This concept, called perspective, is explained beautifully in ALL THOSE SECRETS OF THE WORLD by Jane Yolen, illustrated by Leslie Baker, published by Little, Brown & Co., 1991. In this book, a young girl's father is going far away. Why does his ship look so small? It was so big when he was near.

CHARACTERS CAN BE CHANGED IN A STORY. HERE ARE THREE EXAMPLES...

*THE THREE LITTLE WOLVES AND THE BIG BAD PIG by Eugene Trivizas, illustrated by Helen Oxenbury, published by Macmillan, 1993. A mean, hungry pig is trying to eat three cute, furry wolves. There is another surprise—the safest house is **not** made of bricks!*

DEEP IN THE FOREST illustrated by Brinton Turkle, published by Dutton Children's Books, 1976. In this wordless book, a little bear enters a house. He eats the food, breaks the chair and falls asleep. Uh, oh! Someone is coming home!

YOU CAN'T CATCH ME! by Joanne Oppenheim, illustrated by Andrew Shachat, published by Houghton Mifflin, 1986. A pesky fly is bothering the animals in this book. Who will catch him?

DIFFERENT CULTURES CAN TELL A SIMILAR STORY. HERE'S AN EXAMPLE...

THE KOREAN CINDERELLA by Shirley Climo, illustrated by Ruth Heller, published by HarperCollins, 1993. Omoni and her daughter treat Pear Blossom badly. A frog, birds and an ox magically help her.

THE ROUGH-FACE GIRL by Rafe Martin, illustrated by David Shannon, published by Putnam, 1992. The girl's face has scars and her clothes are rags. The other Algonquin Indians laugh at her. But she has courage, faith in herself and a good, kind heart. Does this "Cinderella" story have a happy ending?

CINDERELLA AND OTHER TALES FROM PERRAULT by Charles Perrault, illustrated by Michael Hague, published by H. Holt and Co., 1989. The Fairy Godmother helps Cinderella go to the ball in this classic version of Cinderella.

A STORY CAN BE MADE INTO A PLAY. HERE'S AN EXAMPLE...

You'll love the creative costumes worn by the children who act out THE STORY OF CHICKEN LICKEN written and illustrated by Jan Ormerod, published by Lothrop, 1986.

Teaching Tips

On the Farm

PIG (page 12) — Just for fun, have the children trace a small leaf for the pig's ear. Do you have a "pig ear" tree or shrub?

SHEEP (page 15) — Describe the head (step 1) as a backward "J". Describe the ear (step 1) as the letter "U".

COW (page 16) — The head (step 1) is shaped like a goblet. See the drawing on the left. This may be a difficult shape for your children to draw. If so, make patterns for the children to trace around or pre-draw the head for them.

HORSE (page 19) — Describe the ears (step 1) as the letter "M" tipped on its side.

BARN (page 23) — The children may enjoy using rulers when drawing barns.

DUCK (page 24) — The children have choices! Are the ducks' bills open or closed? Are the ducks in the water or are they on the land?

TRACTOR (page 28) — Some children may want to draw farmers on the seats of their tractors. Children who live in farm communities may want to draw farm equipment behind their tractors!

Kids and Critters

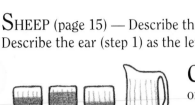

GIRL (page 35) — The eyes (step 4) are drawn in the middle of the head.

SWAN (page 44) — Describe the neck (step 1) as a large number "2" that is tipped a little.

Storybook Characters

THREE LITTLE PIGS (page 54) — Have the children draw three circles (step 1) across the upper portion of their papers for the pigs' heads. Make sure the children space their circles far enough apart to allow room for the pigs' bodies and legs (steps 2, 3 and 4). After drawing the pigs, the children can go back and add their hats and building materials.

THREE BEARS (page 57) — Have the children draw three circles (one small, one medium and one large) for the bears' heads (step 1). After finishing steps 1 through 3, the children can complete their drawings by adding hats and collars to their three bears.

GINGERBREAD BOY (page 58) — Instead of drawing a house at the end of the path (step 4), the children may want to draw an animal (real or imaginary) chasing the Gingerbread Boy. Ask the children to share their versions of the story when they finish their drawings!